BECOMING A
Boss Lady

THE STEP BY STEP GUIDE TO STARTING A BUSINESS

by Belinda Blanding

Copyright © 2019 Belinda Blanding.

All rights reserved. This book or any portion thereof may not be reproduced or used in any matter whatsoever without the express written permission of the Publisher except for the use of brief quotations in a book review.

Published by Belinda Blanding
P.O. Box 1207
New York, NY10008

TABLE OF CONTENTS

Title Page

Copyright Page

Table Of Contents..i

Introduction..ii

Chapter One: Business Idea and Plan....................1

Chapter Two: Choosing and Registering a Business Name...13

Chapter Three: Overcoming Obstacles................25

Chapter Four: Set Up Shop................................35

Chapter Five: Building A Brand..........................43

Chapter Six: Accomplishing Your Goals..............49

Chapter Seven: Let's Get Personal.....................55

Chapter Eight: Keep Pushing..............................61

Chapter Nine: Marketing....................................67

Epilogue..74

About The Author......................................Back Cover

INTRODUCTION

> "I'm a big fan of small business ownership.
> I think it's the backbone of American innovation.
> But to be successful, you first have to have the courage to go for it".
>
> **- Bill Rancic**

Congratulations! You have just made the first step on starting your business. I know that starting a business can be a very scary thing for a beginner. You may not be sure where or even how to begin. Well thats where I come in. I will provide you with all of the tools and resources necessary to start and run a successful business. You have made this purchase which tells me that you are ready to take charge of your life and be in control of your destiny. Whether you are looking to start a full time business or work on your business part time on the side, you are on the right track to pursuing your dreams. Now lets take the bull by the horns and start building your own opportunities.

> "If **opportunity** doesn't knock,
> build a door"
>
> **- Milton Berle**

CHAPTER 1
BUSINESS IDEA AND PLAN

Think Of A Business Idea

For every business there was first an idea. In 1994 Jeff Bezos had an idea to start an online bookstore and named it Amazon. Today Amazon is one of the most if not the most valuable public company in the world, selling **much** more than books these days. In 1985, Thomas G. Stemberg needed a ribbon for his type writer, but because his local small supply store was closed for the holiday, he could not purchase this much needed ribbon. This lead to his brilliant idea to open up a mega supply store so that others like him would not have to rely on small businesses for their supplies. That mega supple store is the store that we all know today as Staples. Both are very successful businesses that all began with a simple idea. Just like many other businesses. They all started with an idea. Now it is your time. What is your idea? I am sure some of you may already have an idea brewing. As for the rest of you I'm guessing that you have a desire to start a business but you're just not sure what type of a business. For you guys, I want you to take a moment to answer these five questions:

1. What is my passion?

_____
_____
_____
_____
_____

2. What is there a need for?

_____
_____
_____
_____
_____

3. What do I enjoy doing?

_____
_____
_____
_____
_____

4. What is my talent or skill?

_____
_____
_____
_____
_____

5. What is my area of expertise?

_____
_____
_____
_____
_____

Examine your answers carefully and determine if any of them give you a business idea. For example: If you enjoy cooking you might want to think about starting a catering service. If you like working with kids, opening up a day care service would be great. If you're like me and have an obsession for shoes, you can start a shoe business. You get the idea. Remember, your business can be anything that provides either a product or a service. My idea came to me very easily. I absolutely love stylish shoes. I also know there are a lot of women like myself who goes gaga over a beautiful pair of shoes. Therefore, when I decided that I wanted to start a business, it was a no brainer. I love shoes, there's a demand for women's shoes by women like myself, why not sell them? I also thought, it would be a great way of getting shoes at a wholesale price for myself. What can be better? Before taking the first step of starting my business I was very aware of the fact that there are shoe stores everywhere. Online shoe stores, shoe boutiques, and many many department stores with shoe departments. In fact, if I'm being honest, I was a little discouraged by the thought of it. Then I thought about the many successful make up lines. The many successful clothing lines, and just in general the many successful retail stores that all sell the exact same items. There's enough success out there for everyone. How many times have you gone to three or more different stores looking for the perfect dress? What one store doesn't have, the next one may have. Whether it's the style, color or size. Consumers need options. The more options they have the better for them. With that said never worry about how many people are already doing it. It is your business so make it your own.

What ever business idea you decide on, be sure that it is something that you enjoy. This is important because starting and running a business is not always peaches and cream. There will be some good and bad days, but if its something that you enjoy doing, that will help to keep you going. If nothing else, you're WHY is really what will keep you strong when times get tough. Why are you starting a business? That is the one simple most important question that you must ask yourself before starting your business. Once you know what your why is, when the business has you feeling like giving up, you'll think back to why you started it. That always seemed to have worked for me. I want you all to take a moment and write down below your *why*.

I AM STARTING MY BUSINESS BECAUSE…..

_____
_____
_____
_____
_____

Businesses usually fall into four separate categories. Once you have your idea, you should pretty much know what type of business your business falls under. The following are the four different types of businesses. Which one will you have?

Service: This type of business is when you help or do work for someone. Usually providing your skills, expertise, and or your time.

The following three types of businesses are all related to providing a product:

Manufacturing: This is the production of merchandise or

goods with the intent to be sold. Manufacturers usually do not deal directly with the consumer.

Wholesale: The Wholesaler purchases products or goods from the manufacturer and sells it to the Retailer or other Wholesalers. Like the Manufacturer, the Wholesaler does not usually deal directly with the consumer.

Retail: The retailer sells goods and merchandise directly to the consumer. Retailing is the last and final link in the supply chain.

Now that you have your business idea, established the type of business, and identified your why, let's now get into how to make your idea come to fruition.

Research! Research! Research! You must do your research and find out if there are any special skills or qualifications that are required before starting your business. For example, if you want to open up your own hair salon, you first must go to school for Cosmetology and receive your license. For most businesses there are no special requirements. All that will be required is your hard work and dedication. You may still want to do a little research just to get a clearer idea of what starting and running that particular business would entail. In doing your research, you will most likely come across terms you may not fully understand or be familiar with. Some terms you may be familiar with but maybe not in relation to running a business. Before starting a business you should try to familiarize yourselves with the Business Terminology. I will list and define below the most used business terms and what you should know as a business owner.

Business Terms

Accounting

This is the recording and reporting of your businesses financial transactions. There are different accounting and bookkeeping apps that you can use for small businesses such as Quickbooks Accounting, GoDaddy Bookkeeping, and EZBooks-Mobile Bookkeeping. If you will have a larger company, accounting may become a little more complicated and I would recommend hiring an Accountant in that case. Keeping track of your business finances for tax filing purposes. It is very important that you keep accurate records.

Accounts Receivable

Accounts Receivable is the amount of money that your customers or clients owe to your business for goods or services provided to them. Whenever you need to know the total dollar amount owed to your business at any given time, you can take a glance at your accounts receivable number.

Accounts Payable

Accounts Payable is a measure of how much you owe your creditors for goods or services that they have supplied you with.

Assets

This is your business' financial cumulative financial holdings. Assets are either current or or fixed. Current, or short-term assets include cash or inventory. Fixed, or long-term assets include equipment or land.

Liabilities

Liabilities are debts your business owes to another person or entity. Liabilities are also defines by either current or fixed. Current, or short-term liabilities may include expensed payable to a supplier. Most business loans are long-term debs.

Revenue

Revenue refers to the income you get from a business activity at any time. Revenue is calculated by multiplying the per-unit cost to the goods or services by the quantity of units sold.

Owner's Equity

Owner's Equity is what the owner's part of the business assets is referred to. It is usually represented as a percentage.

Balance Sheet

The Balance Sheet is a financial document which provides a snapshot of the business' assets, liabilities, and owner's equity.

Bottom Line

Also known as "net profit". Bottom line represents the total revenues minus the total expenses. This number is especially important when it's time to file your taxes. That's because you pay self-employment taxes as a percentage of net profit.

Net Loss

This is when your total expenses exceed your total revenues. When that happens, you have a net loss. You must keep your company costs under control to prevent this from happening.

Profit Margin

This basically tells you how much profit you get to keep relative to total sales. There are three types of profit margins. Gross, operating, and net. Calculate these by dividing the profit, which is the revenue minus the costs, by the revenue.

Cash Flow

Cash Flow is the movement of money in and out of your business. Your goal is to have more money flowing into the business as opposed to having an outflow of expenses from the business, which is called a positive cash flow.

Return On Investment

Your return on investment (ROI) is what shows you how much you've gained or lost on an investment relative to how much you've spent on it. ROI is calculated by dividing your net profit by the cost of your investment.

Capitol

Capitol is simply what your company has of value such as cash or assets.

E-Commerce

This is the process of doing business over the internet. If you plan on having an online store, that would be an example of an E-Commerce business.

Gross Sales

Gross Sales is the total amount of sales before any expenses are deducted.

Expenses

This is how much money it will cost you to run and operate your business on a regular basis. Expenses include, the purchases of products and goods, rent if you run your business from an office or commercial space, marketing, etc.

Call To Action (CTA)

This is when you prompt customers or potential customers to do something. For example, "Open up an account and receive 10% off of your order".

I know this is a lot and trust me there's a lot more but I don't want to take up much more time on this. I just want to make sure that you know and are familiar with the most used business terms. Once you start your business and begin running it, you will learn more as you go along as I did. I unfortunately had to learn and research as I went along. Now that I know and understand the business, I want to share my knowledge with you so that you will have what I'll call a "blueprint" to refer to. Which is something that I wish that I had.

CHAPTER 2
CHOOSING AND REGISTERING A BUSINESS NAME

Choosing Your Business Name

Choosing your business name is probably one of the most important decision regarding your business that you will make. Your business name plays a role in just about every aspect of your business. So make sure that it's short, easy to pronounce, trendy, and most importantly, that it conveys what you do. It can be something as simple as "Bob's Tire Repair". It is straight to the point. He's Bob and his business is repairing tires. No confusion there. You can always be a little more creative when choosing your business name. For example, my shoe business name is Divalynn Shoetique. Here is the break down of how I came up with the name. Diva comes from what I am often described as by many, so I took it and ran with it. Next, I took a part of my first name, which is how I got lynn. I changed the spelling because it just looked better. Lastly, my store is an online shoe boutique, so I combined the words shoe and boutique to get shoetique. There you have Divalynn Shoetique. That's just to give you an idea on ways to come up with a good name.

Now that you have your name you must secure your domain name. Your domain name is your business's unique identity. Every business should invest in a domain name especially if you are planning to have an internet presence. Your domain will allow people to find your business on the internet. An example of a domain name would be divalynnshoetique.com or divalynnshoetique.net. I recommend purchasing your name from GoDaddy.com. It's about $30 a year and you have the option of paying for two or more years at a time. The other good thing about GoDaddyis that it will not allow you to purchase a domain that is already in use. You would have to type in the search bar your desired business name. GoDaddy instantly lets you know if that name is taken and will not allow you to use it. Can you imagine thinking of the perfect business name, setting up your business, and investing a lot of money into it, just to later find out someone is using that same business name? This will not happen if you do a business name search with GoDaddy first. Upon check out you will also be given the option of purchasing the matching email address for an additional fee. I highly recommend doing so. Yahoo and Gmail are great but having your own company's name as your email account gives your business a more professional look and feel. An example of a matching email address would be Belindablanding@divalynnshoetique.com. Also, it's great if you wish to have separate emails for each employee if you are going to have employees. You can even have a separate email address for different departments. Customersupport@divalynnshoetique.com and info@divalynnshoetique.com for example. Again, I highly recommend using GoDaddy. You'll be able to set up your domain, email, and even set up your website. We will talk about websites in a later chapter.

Registering Your Business Name

You have chosen your name now it's time to register it. This is where you begin the formalizing of your business. Here I am going to go into full detail on the importance of registering your business name and the different options available. Registering your name is not only required by law but it s for your own protection as well. When you register your business name no one else can use it or do business under your company's name. You want to be sure that when customers do a search for Bob's Tire Repair, they find you and you only. Also, just imagine if someone has your same name and doing business horribly. Now you have a bad reputation due to someone else using your business name. You don't want that to happen so please register your business name so that no one can come behind you and use your name.

There are three different ways that you can **Register Your Business Name.** I have listed them below.

1. Use a Doing Business As (DBA): Filing a DBA with your state or county clerk's office is the easiest way to register a business. This is also the most common method used by Sole Proprietors. Sole Proprietor is one of the four business structures that you will have to choose from. I will go into details later about the four options to choose from as well as the advantages and disadvantages of each. Now back to DBA. An example of using a Doing Business As (DBA) would be if Susan Jones owns a flower shop, she may file a Doing Business As "Jones Flower Shop". All of her business documents would have to read "Susan Jones DBA Jones Flower Shop". If you are using your own name as your business name there is no need to register your business name.

2. Create A Business Structure: Creating a business structure is the most common way that people register their business names. An example of a business structure would be when your company is registered as an LLC or

Corporation. Creating an LLC or Corporation would actually be like killing two birds with one stone. You are setting up your business structure and in doing so you are also registering your business name at the same time.

3. Register a Trademark: To register a trademark you must file an application with the United States Patent and Trademark Office. This will Trademark your name with the federal government. If your business name has been trademarked by a similar name, your application will be denied and your fee will not be refunded. So again, I stress the importance of doing a search before choosing your business name to be sure it isn't already in use.

If you need assistance registering your business name I highly recommend using Legal Zoom. I have and continue to use Legal Zoom for most of my business needs. Legal Zoom can help you with filing a DBA, creating a business structure, and registering a trademark. Their website is very user friendly. You just pick what it is you are trying to do and you will be lead to the appropriate form to fill out right online. Legal Zoom will do all of your filing by sending all of the appropriate documents to your state and/or County Clerk's office. Once everything is done, they will send to you by mail of the documents you will need, which you will keep in a safe place for your records. You will not have to do any of the filing yourself.

I myself, opted to creating a business structure to register my business name. An LLC to be exact. In case some of you are under the impression that a sole business owner must file as a Sole Proprietor, that is false. As a sole business owner you can choose from several business structures. Creating a business structures is the most popular method of registering a business name. As I mentioned earlier, I am going to go into the different business structures there are to choose from.

Types of Business Structures

Sole Proprietor: Is when a business is owned and run entirely by one individual. The owner is in direct control and also is solely responsible and accountable for all of the business finances. That includes debt and any and all losses. Although a Sole Proprietor is owned and operated by one individual that does not mean that they work alone necessarily. A sole proprietor may at any point and time hire people to work for their company.

Advantage

* Easy and inexpensive to set up and register business name.

* Owner has full control of business.
* Owner receives all profits. Does not have to divide profits.
* Fewer reports have to be filed with government agencies.

Disadvantage

* Owner carries the sole financial responsibility for all debts and losses suffered by the business.
* Owner's personal assets such as bank accounts and property can be used to discharge any outstanding liabilities.
* Business owner is solely responsible for all business activities conducted by their employees
* Less capital available since an individual's resources are less are less than the pooled resources of a partnership.

Partnerships (General and Limited): A general partnership is an agreement between two or more individuals who join together to enter a business venture. Not only does each partner contribute their labor, skill, and money, each also shares in the profit and losses of the business.

Each partner has unlimited liability personal liability for the debts of the business. A limited partnership limits the personal liability of each partner for the debts and losses of the business.

Advantage

* More capital availability
* More support, more than one person making all of the decisions, which makes decision making less stressful.
* Partners are not financially responsible for the debts and losses occurred by the other partners.

Disadvantage

* Partners are personally responsible for all debts and losses. A lien can be placed on personal assets or can be seized to recover outstanding balances.
* Partners have equal authority when it comes to making business decisions which can lead to disagreements. Disagreements may lead to delays or even the ending of the partnership.
* In some states a limited partnership may be limited to certain professionals such as doctors and lawyers. Check with your state first if a limited partnership is a consideration.

Limited Liability Company (LLC): Businesses structured as an LLC has a lot of similarities to businesses structured as a limited partnership. A lot of individual owners who own their businesses alone, without a partner, opt to form an LLC because of it's limited liability protection, which protects the individual's personal assets.

Advantage:

* Owner has limited financial responsibility for debts and loss suffered by the business.
* Owner's personal assets cannot be seized to cover any of the businesses outstanding liabilities.
* An owner that has sole ownership has the benefits of a sole proprietor but has limited liability.
* Under an LLC structure, your business can be a corporation, a partnership, or have just one business owner. You're not restricted to being one or the other under an LLC.

Disadvantage:

* Profits may be subject to self employment taxes.

Corporations: A Corporation is a company or a group of people authorized to act as a single legal entity that is separated from its owners. A corporation is owned by its shareholder(s), who elects a board of directors to oversee the organization's activities.

Advantage:

* Corporations provide liability protection for its owners (shareholders).
* It is easier for corporations to raise money from investors because they have shares that can be sold.

* Working for a corporation is more appealing to potential employees than working for a small company making it easier to hire needed help.

Disadvantage:

* Corporations or harder and more complex to set up.
* Corporations spend lots of time and money to stay on top of regulations that are continuously changing.
* Unlike the other business structures, which mostly pay only state taxes, corporations pay federal, state, and sometimes local taxes on their earnings.

So there you have it! The four business structures. It is very important and advantageous for you to know what all of them are as well as the pros and cons of each. You will eventually have to decide (if you haven't already), which one you be will forming for your business. If you will be running your business alone, I highly recommend that you file your business as an LLC as opposed to a Sole Proprietor. As a sole proprietor, you have no protection over your personal assets. Lets say that one day a customer decides to file a law suit against you for whatever reason. If you are a sole proprietor, they can go after your house, bank accounts, etc. If you are an LLC, they can only go after your business assets. That's just to give you an example of the protection having an LLC would give you.

In the end, I want you to do what is best for you and your business. Which ever business structure you end up going with, I recommend using Legal Zoom. They can help you to set up your business structure, do your filing, and send you all required documents. Also, most importantly, if you need to know what, if any licenses or permits you are required to have for your business, Legal Zoom can help you with that as well. Based on the type of business you're starting, and by answering a few questions, they will tell you exactly what you need to apply for. You would think that Legal Zoom is paying me by the way that I keep mentioning them. Actually, I just want you guys to get your businesses up and running smoothly just the way it was for me. When I feel like something was very helpful for me, I am always more than happy to share the information. I want you all to succeed and with the proper resources, the road to success would make it that much easier. At the end of this book, you will find a list of many different resources that you may find helpful throughout your starting up process. I hope they will be as helpful to you as they were for me.

CHAPTER 3
OVERCOMING OBSTICLES

Now that you know the basics on how to start your business, I have one question to ask. Are you ready? If you are ready to rock and roll, great! If not, what is holding you back? What is stopping you from taking that first step? Most people believe that in order to start a business they need a whole lot of money. Well that all depends on the type of business that you are starting. Don't get me wrong, the start up costs for certain businesses can be quite expensive. If you are starting a business that require an office space or a any other physical location, you will have to consider the cost of leasing that space. You will need to perhaps furnish that space and/or purchase certain equipment. Then there's your inventory if you are opening a store that sells products and merchandise. You will surely need to have a large inventory when first starting out. These are just a few things that you will have to consider when starting a business that has a physical location. On the other hand, if you are staring a business that provides a service only, such as a business as a Personal Training, Health and Fitness expert, or a Life Coach, the start up cost would be little to none. There is usually no inventory needed, and you don't have to have a physical location such as an office or a store, unless you choose to. If you do wish to start a business in sales, meaning a business that provides a product or merchandise, there is another option than opening up a store. You may want to start a business selling clothing, shoes, sneakers, books, etc., but do not have access to the up front funds that is needed, you can opt to start an online business. It may not be what your ultimate goal is, however, it is a start. Starting an online business will get your business started, build your clientele, and get your name out there. Once you start earning enough profit, you will eventually be able to save up enough money to pen up the store at that shop you've been dreaming of. In the next chapter I will into more details about the location options of your business, including online business as well as storefront businesses. If you have your mind set that you want to start a business that requires leasing space, buying inventory, etc., and you do not wish to do an online business, I will give you a few options to look into. Staring with an online business may not be an option for everyone. You might be a person that prefers to have one on one contact with your customers or clients. It also isn't an option if your starting a business such as a child care business or any type of service that would be impossible to provide online. Here are some options for you if the start up costs are a little more than you can afford right now.

Apply For a Business Loan

Applying for a business loan is one route that you can take. You make an investment in your education when taking out a student loan. Why not invest in your dream by taking out a business loan. When applying for a business loan, the banks do look at your credit score as one of the factors in determining your eligibility. I suggest that you have a credit score of at least 640. Higher is of course better, but if you have anything less than that your chances of getting approved are very slim. To increase your score, I would suggest making sure you make all of your monthly payments on time every month. You should also keep your credit card balances below thirty percent of the limit. For example, if your credit card has a $5,000 limit, your outstanding balance should not be more than $3,500. Creditors look at how you use your credit. Therefore, keep your balances as low as possible. If you don't have any credit or very little credit, that is also looked upon negatively. I would suggest applying for two or three secured credit cards. A secured credit card is when you deposit your own money (after approved), into the account and you would receive a credit card with the amount that you deposited available. You can deposit as little as $200.00. You will use the card by making small purchases then paying them off right away. As you do this, you are developing a good credit history. The bank that you received your card from will report to the three major credit reporting agencies of your good standing. By doing all of the above over a certain amount of time, I would say six months to a year, your credit score will surely increase. Once you are comfortable with your credit score you can prepare yourself for the next step. When applying for a business loan you will need to develop a strong business plan to present to the bank or investor. A business plan should should be.outlined to include six very important components. The first is:

1. *Opportunity:* In this section of your business plan it describes what it is that you're selling and how your products and services will fill a need for your customers. Basically, you are describing the problem that the customers have and the solution that you are selling or providing.

2. *Market Analysis Summary:* You must know your target market. Such as the types of customers you are looking for. Here is where you will discuss who your target customers and clients are, their needs, and how you will deliver your

product or service to them. Here is where in your business plan you will also discuss how will you fit into the market. With so many other similar businesses, you must show how you will stack up against the competitors and discuss why you are confident that there is room for you in this market.

3. *Execution:* In this part of your business plan, you will go into detail on how you plan on successfully running your business. You will outline your your sales plan as well as your marketing plan. You will need to also include the location you will be running your business from as well as any equipment if any, that you will be needing. You should also outline in this section your key metrics that you'll be using to insure that your business is headed down the right track.

4. *Company and Management Summary:* This is the section where you will give an overview of who you are and what is your business. You will include information such as, the names of the owner(s), where you will be conduction business, what state is your business registered in, and the structure of your business. We discussed the different business structures in the last chapter. If your company will have managers that you plan on hiring, you will include their background and experience. You should also include what their duties and responsibilities will be in your

company. I suggest also attaching their resumes to the business plan.

5. *Financial Plan:* This section is very basic. Here is where you should include your projected profit, loss, and cash flow. If you are raising money or taking out loans for the business, here is where you would breakdown how much it is going to cost you to launch the business and how much you will need.

6. *Executive Summary:* In this section you will discuss the highlight of your business plan. This is where you can summarize the problems of the customers, your solutions, and your target market. Keep things short and to the point, yet interesting . I should let you know that your Executive Summary is what will make or break your business plan so make it a good one. Just keep these two words in mind when outlining this section, which are, highlight and summarize.

Open Up a Line Of Credit

Opening up a line of credit is another option you may consider. Just like with applying for a business loan, your credit should be at least a 640 in order to be considered for approval. A credit card with a credit card company would be useful for purchasing inventory, equipment, office furniture, etc. You can even open up a line of credit with specific stores individually. For example, if you will be working from an office, you may want to think about opening a Staples account for your office supplies and furniture.

Find an Investor or Partner

You have this great business idea that you are confident will be successful. You are ready and eager to start but the one thing holding you back is the lack of funds that your particular type of business needs to get started. If you are confident in your business idea, think of someone that you know who has the funds and may be willing to partner up with you. When or if you find that person, come up with an agreement that you both can agree on and please put it in writing. They will provide the funds and you will do all of the leg work required to start and run the business. In return you may offer them a small percentage of your profits. Keep in mind that a partnership does not always have be an equal partnership. Instead of fifty/fifty it can be sixty/forty for example. Whatever the agreement is just be sure to make it a written contract. Maybe you are not interested in being in a partnership. Another alternative is to instead of asking them to be a partner is to ask them to be an investor. They would still help you with the funding but instead of being a partner, you would simply pay them back what they invested with interest. You would have a written contract that would outline how much is to be funded, how much is to be returned, and in how much time will you have to pay it back. Most investors will give you at least one year to pay back the funds. Once your business is up, running, and making profit, you can simply pay back a percentage of your profit till paid in full. An investor does not have to be someone that you know. I know that some of you may not want to or don't feel comfortable asking a friend or family member to invest in your business. There are a lot of investors out there just looking for something good to invest in. It is what they do for a living. If you would prefer finding an outside investor or even if you would prefer applying for a business loan, I recommend that you contact Small Business Administration (SBA). They can assist you with writing a business plan, applying for a business loan, or finding an investor for you. Just look them up online.

Save Your Coins

The last and final option is good old fashioned saving. If you are serious about investing in your dream you will have to make a lot of sacrifices and just save. Discipline yourself and think about the bigger picture, the light at the end of the rainbow, and the benefits that will come from your sacrifices. It will be hard but you can do it! Pick a set amount that you can afford to put into your savings account every time you get paid. Prepare your meals for the week as opposed to buying breakfast and lunch every day. You'll be surprised how much you can save with that alone. If you spend at least fifteen dollars a day buying outside food, five days a week, fifty-two weeks a year, that comes out to $3900 a year. Wow. Instead of hanging out after work once a week, limit it to once or twice a month. When you get your tax return instead of splurging put that money into your savings to go towards your business. Those are just a few ideas but I'm sure that if you are serious about your dream, you can come up with many more.

I hope that the options that I have given you were helpful. There is always a way to overcome your obstacles. "Where there's a will there's a way".

CHAPTER 4
SET UP SHOP

Now it is time to decide on your business location. Will you have a physical location? Such as an office, retail space, or work out of your home? Will you have an online business? These are the questions that you must ask yourself. It is very important for the successful operation of your business that you properly set it up. You will also need to figure out things like, whether or not you will be needing any special equipment or supplies. If you are starting a business in sales of any kind, you are surely going to be needing a good amount of inventory to get started. Think about and decide on how much inventory you want to start off with. You don't have to go broke buying a whole lot of inventory in the beginning. You can start off buying just enough to open up your business. You can do a trial period to see what items sell more, which ones sell less, what your customers are asking for, etc. Once you start making sales you can always reinvest those funds to purchase more inventory (Rule of thumb: Reinvest half of your profit and pay yourself the other half). At least by then you will have an idea of what items sell more, and most importantly, what items are more in demand. When have this information, it is less likely that you will waste money purchasing inventory that will not sell and will just end up collecting dust. When purchasing inventory, always be sure to start off with at least a couple of each of the variants. Variants are things such as colors and sizes. For example, if you are selling dresses that come in three colors and five different sizes, make sure you have a few in each color as well as a few in all five sizes. The reason is, you want to have something for everyone's needs and wants. Of course there will be certain sizes, colors, etc. that will sell out quicker than others. In that case you will have disappointed customers that won't find their size or color. This is something that is unavoidable. The only thing you can do is reorder what is sold out as soon as possible and let your customers know that they can check back at a later time.

If you are starting a business in sales you may either open up a physical store location or you may opt to open up an online store. With an online store you have the option of storing your inventory in your home or hiring a dropshipper. A dropshipping company is a company that stores, sell, and ship the merchandise for you. How it works is, lets say you want to start an online sneaker store. You would do your research and try to find a dropshipping company that sells sneakers. You would contact them, take a look at their website, and see if they sell the type of sneakers that you would be interested in selling on your online store. If so, you would sign up with them and agree to their terms. Every company has their own policies. Then you will be able to advertise their products on your online store. They normally allow you to use their photos as well as their item descriptions. When a customer pays for the item on your store the money goes to you. You will then pay your dropshipper to ship off the item to your customer. When you are paying the dropshipper, you are paying them for the cost of the item, which is charged to you at a wholesale price, and the cost of shipping. I can give you a quick example of how that works. Lets say you are selling a pair of sneakers that the dropshipper has listed at a retail price of $80.00. However, the wholesale price for you is $45.00. The customer orders the sneakers from your website for $80.00, then you pay the wholesale price of $45.00 to the dropshipper. Subtract that $45.00 from the $80.00 that your customer paid you and you have made a profit of $35.00 for the pair of sneakers.

There are several reasons you may choose dropshipping as opposed to shipping yourself. You may not have the available funds needed to purchase the required amount of inventory. You may not have the space in your home to store all of the merchandise. Lastly, you might not have the time to process orders and ship them out yourself. Dropshipping would be your best choice if any of the above mentioned applies to you. I also want you to keep in mind that where there are advantages, there also comes disadvantages. Here are some of the disadvantages of dropshipping. One is you do not have full control over your business. If someone else is shipping items to your customer, you have no idea what condition the item may be in that is being sent. You don't know if they are sending the correct item. Lastly, and most importantly, you don't know if your customer's order was even sent out. Eventually, you will know when you receive an email or message from an angry customer. The unfortunate thing is if any of these things happen, your business now has a bad reputation due to the fault of your dropshipper and not yours. The customer just sees your name and business. They're not interested nor are they concerned about a dropshipper. I myself, have had the opportunity to work with a dropshipping company. I have had for the most part a good experience. However, there were a couple of mishaps here and there. One mishap is actually one too many. Again, it is the reputation of your business that is on the line. I have since been connected to a fashion wholesaler that I absolutely love. They have great clothes, shoes, and accessories, for both men and women at great wholesale prices. I have ordered my women's shoes and accessories from them and I love them. I store the items in my home and ship them myself. This is something you can do as well. You can find a great wholesaler that sells whatever it is that you are interested in selling and order your merchandise from them. If you're concerned about storage space you can maybe thing about renting out a storage space. Maybe you have an extra room in your home or an empty garage. If you have a basement, you can probably find space there. I'm sure you'll come up with something. As far as shipping, you can pick one or two days a week where you can focus on packaging and shipping orders. Please do not attempt to process orders as soon as you get them especially if you are working alone. You will drive yourself insane. It's best to pick a couple of days each week to process orders. Which consists of boxing, applying shipping labels, and dropping off to the post office. You may want to purchase a shipping label printer along with a scale for weighing packages. They are both very inexpensive. Once your packages are packed and labeled, as I mentioned, you can load up your vehicle, if you have one, or get a ride, and drop your packages off at the post office. If that's not something you want to do, you can schedule a pick up with the post office. The post office will come and pick up your packages, regardless of how many, and take them to the post office for you. You will just have to pick a specific date and time for them to come. As I said you might want to do this a couple of times per week.

Now on the other hand, you may be starting a business that doesn't provide a product but provides a service. A service can be anything such as a childcare provider, Personal Trainer, or Real Estate Broker. The great thing about a business that provides a service, is that there is no inventory involved. In fact, for most businesses that provides a service, a business location isn't necessary either. For example, a life coach, personal trainer, or fitness expert, can do business without needing an office or having inventory. A website, access to the internet, and a phone is all that is needed to get started. However, if you are starting a business that requires an office or retail space, you will have a little more work to do. The first thing you will need to do is find a location to lease. When looking for the space to lease, keep in mind that location is a very important factor when opening a business. The location of your business can be one of the reasons why your business succeeds or fails. You don't want to open up your shoe store across the street from another shoe store. Also, you don't want to set up shop in a deserted area where people are not frequently walking by. Most businesses get there business from a passerby. With that said make sure your business is in a busy area. Once you have secured your location, you will not have to furnish it. If it is an office, you will need desks, chairs, computers, etc. If is a retail location you will just mostly need your inventory and perhaps a couple of chairs. I suggest that when shopping for your space, that you try to find a place that is already furnished and set up for the business. For example, for your shoe store, try to find an actual shoe store space for rent. It will already have the shoe shelves and everything a shoe store is required to have. For your office, try to find an actual office space for rent. It would more than likely already have the desks, chairs, etc. This way you will just make your down payment and move on in.

Whether you will be starting a business that offers a product or a service, an online store or a physical store, you should advertise and announce your launch date. Let people know that you have a business and that it will be launching soon. Announce the date so everyone can be prepared and be ready to support your business.

CHAPTER 5
BUILDING A BRAND

Now that your business is up and running, it is time to start building your brand. Your brand is what separates you from similar businesses. It is how you let your customers and clients know the reason for your existence. Your brand will include everything about your business such as your logo, your theme colors, your slogan, etc. No matter what type of business you have, you want to build a brand that your customers and clients can trust. Your brand is your business' reputation whether good or bad. Whether you want to accept it or not, people do judge. That's what they do. It is human nature. With that said, your business will be judged. It's appearance, your customer service, the quality of your service or products, and what your business stands for. Let's start with what your business stands for. You will let your customers and clients know what you stand for with your mission statement. Your mission statement is a huge part of your brand. Your mission statement should give a clear statement on your company's values and purposes.

Next, let us talk about the appearance of your company. This is where your logo, theme colors, and organization come in. Choose a logo that coincides with your brand, company name, and colors. The colors that you choose will be your own personal choice. You can choose colors that you think will make your business stand out, or you can simply choose your favorite colors. I myself, am absolutely obsessed with pink. Therefore, my brand colors are pink, white, and black. Whatever colors you decide to go with is totally up to you. You also want to be sure that you are organized. Nothing turns a potential customer off more than not being able to find anything. Whether you have a physical store or an online store, everything should be organized and easy to locate and navigate through. Your website should be user friendly and easy to work through without confusion. If a potential customer goes on your website and finds is difficult to get around or can't get to what they're looking for within the first sixty seconds, they will log off. Which will mean losing a customer. Since we are on the subject of websites, I think now is a good time to talk about creating a bomb website. Every business should have a website whether you are selling merchandise or not. Even if you have a business that provides a service or information, having a great website is an important part of your business. A website is where you get to talk about your business. You can let people know what you do and what you have to offer. This way your customer will have an idea of what you're all about. It is also a place to display and sell your products if you are in sales. You're website should always match your brand. For example, your website should display your logo, it should include your slogan (if you have one), and it's color scheme should be the same as your brand colors. Your website should also include your mission statement. A business website is like is like a cyber resume. It is where people will find out who you are, what you do, and what you have to offer. Therefore, make it a good one.

The quality of your products also plays an important part of your branding. You should have quality merchandise that fits the needs of your customers. Quality is very important. Remember this is your reputation that is on the line. Your products should always be in perfect condition without any damage. The materials used in making the merchandise should always be of good quality and priced accordingly.

The most important part of your branding is customer service. I cannot emphasize that enough. People will always remember how you made them feel. You may have the best products or the best prices around, but if you possess poor customer service, none of that will matter. What you don't want to do is lose business because of the quality of your customer service. Here is a news flash: Your customers hold your reputation in the palm of their hands. If a customer is displeased with your business you can believe that will let everyone know who will listen. They can leave bad reviews or even report you to the Better Business Bureau, depending on the level of the complaint. With that in mind, your main objective should be to please the customers. Without them, you have no business. They are the consumers. The ones you need to support your business. You should always be polite and courteous. Always try to be as helpful as possible when a problem or complaint arises. If there's an issue with a product or service, always offer a an alternative to rectify the issue. Most importantly, listen to your customers. Listen to their concerns and issues. When you listen, it shows the customer that you respect their thoughts and opinions and are open to suggestions. It will keep them coming back to you.

Let me share a personal example with you. My online shoe store Divalynn Shoetique has been doing well. However, I have received some feedback from customers as well as potential customers regarding my prices. That they were a bit high, which I do agree that they were. Unfortunately, the prices were set by the company that supplied me with the merchandise and it was out of my control. What I did was, I shopped around to find other suppliers with more reasonable prices. I was fortunate enough to locate a couple and got rid of my old supplier. In between changing suppliers, I had to temporarily pause my website to allow time to get all of my new merchandise and display them on my website. I did that not for me, but for my customers and potential customers. I wanted to be affordable for everyone. It all comes down to keeping them happy and coming back. Another very important part of building your brand is building a brand that your customers can trust. In order to gain your customers trust, you have to be true to your word and do whatever it is that you promised your customers as a business. Do what you say you are going to do and be who and what you said your company would be. In other words, deliver on your promises. If you say a product will be shipped within three days, make sure that product ships within three days. If you say you'll respond to their email within twenty-four hours, respond to their email within twenty-four hours. Remember the old saying "My word is my bond"? Lets change that to "My word is my brand". Do what you say you're going to do. Simple. Do not give anyone the ammunition to give you a bad reputation. Remember this very profound quote by Jeff Bezos,

Founder of Amazon, "Your Brand is what other people say about you when you're not in the room". When people speak about your business and your brand you want them to speak positively about it, even when you are not in the room. You want them to spread the word about your business and have nothing but good things to say about you and your business.

Make your brand stand out from the rest. What is going to be special about your brand that will make customers choose you? Take a moment to think about some of your favorite places to shop or do business. Why do you frequently give them your business when you have so many other options to choose from? Is it their merchandise? Is it their customer service? Or is it what they stand for? It may even be something as simple as a logo that stands out to you. When answering these questions, think about what you can do to give your customers that same feeling to continue coming to you.

CHAPTER 6
ACCOMPLISHING YOUR GOALS

It is very important to always set goals and work towards accomplishing them. As a business owner, you should be continuously setting and working hard to achieve them. You have to have something that you are working towards, something that will keep you motivated. In this chapter I will be giving you ten steps to setting and accomplishing your goals.

Step 1: What are your goals? You will need to establish what exactly are your goals. What do you want? What do you need? Where do you see your business in the next six months or year. How much profit would you like to see yourself making? What are your short term goals? What are your long term goals? Those are the sort of questions you should be asking yourself.

Step 2: Write them down. Once you know what your goals are, the next step would be to write them them.

"An idea is just a dream until you write it down, then it is a goal" - Anonymous

I would like you to take this moment to briefly write down some of your short term goals. Just to get into the habit of writing them down. Think carefully about it and write down exactly what goals you would like to achieve in the near future. Keep this list handy and glance at in every now and then just to remind yourself of your goals and where you are as far as accomplishing them.

My Goals Are To:

_____

_____

_____

_____

_____

_____

_____

_____

Having your goals written down on paper makes it a real. You now have something tangible that you can look at and remind yourself and to stay on track. Always keep your written goals in a safe place where you can easily access them. I personally write my goals down in a small spiral notebook and keep it in the nightstand beside by bed. I, like many people do most of my thinking when its bedtime. I lie in bed and all sorts of thoughts and ideas pop into my head. When that happens, which is often, I can just reach over and pull the book out of my nightstand drawer and start writing. Other times, I might just want to look over my goals quickly before going to bed. You don't have to do what I do, but do what works best for you. If you choose to write your goals down on one hundred little post its, if thats what works for you that is fine. The point is that they are written down.

Step 3: Set attainable goals. Make sure you set goals that are realistic. Setting unrealistic goals will only lead to failure, disappointment, and discouragement. Don't be confused between setting unrealistic goals and setting challenging goals. Your should always set challenging goals. Challenging, yet attainable goals should be your objective.

Step 4: Set a deadline. When setting a goal, it is important to set a deadline. Otherwise, procrastination can set in, and one goal will take forever to complete if you complete it at all. If you have a date written down, that will give you the motivation to keep going so that you can reach your goal in time. If you are competitive with yourself like I am, you will be sure to meet that deadline. If it is a big goal to complete, give yourself enough time. The worst thing that you can do is set an unrealistic goal or overwhelm yourself. You can also break the goal down into separate steps and set a deadline for each step.

Step 5: Write out a plan. Writing down your goals is a must. However, simply writing them down is not enough. You also have to write out how you plan on achieving those goals. For example, if your goal is to make one thousand sales this month, just writing down that you want to make one thousand sales this month won't help much. You have to know what is is that you need to do to achieve that goal. What would it entail? Maybe it entails changes in your marketing system, increasing the amount of time you invest into your business, etc. Once you list the steps that it will take to reach those goals, it becomes more reachable. You know what you want to do and exactly what it is you need to do to make it happen.

Step 6: Take that first step. Starting anything is always difficult. The first step is always the hardest step to make. You can talk the talk but it means nothing until you actually walk the walk. You can list your goals, you can write down how you plan on achieving those goals, which is the easy part. Now it is time to put those words into actions. After taking the first step, the following steps will flow naturally and easily. However, whatever you do, do not stop. Once you stop, starting over will be just as difficult as it was to initially start in the beginning.

Step 7: Work on your goals every day. Do something everyday to work towards your goal. Whether you spend twenty minutes or two hours each day, doing something every day is moving you closer to achieving your goals. If you have time to watch your favorite television shows, time to spend on social media everyday, you have time to invest some time every day in your dream. Remember that consistency is key. "Success doesn't come from what you do occasionally, it comes from what you do consistently" - Marie Forleo.

Step 8: Never give up. If you must, take a break, rest, catch your second wind, then get right back on it. Do what you must but do not give up. You are closer now to your goal than you were before you got started. Keep going! You are almost there. The worst thing you can do is give up when you are so close to reaching your goal. Hang in there. You got this!

Step 9: Reward yourself. Congratulations! You have

completed a goal. For every goal that you have completed, you should reward yourself. Why not? You've worked hard. You stayed focused, committed, and disciplined. You deserve it. Rewarding yourself gives you an incentive to keep going. Knowing that you have something to look forward to at the end of completion, makes staying focused a piece of cake. This step can be used toward achieving any goals, not just business goals. This is actually something that I do pretty often.

Step 10: Set your next set of goals. At this point you should overwhelmed with the feeling of satisfaction. You have now proven to yourself that with hard work, commitment, and dedication, you can do anything that you set your mind to. Now you should have the confidence and the ambition to keep reaching for the stars. You should always be looking for new goals to set. Never become complacent. There is always room to grow. You don't have to start on your new goals right away. If you need to, you can take a break between your goals. Just a break but don't stop creating and working on new goals.

CHAPTER 7
LETS GET PERSONAL

Thinking back to the time before I launched Divalynn Shoetique, I didn't have a clue as to where or how to begin. I had no knowledge on how to start a business let alone run a one. I had to do a lot of research and a lot of reading. I knew that if this was something that I wanted to come to fruition, I would have to put in the work. My goal was to create a business doing something that I enjoy. I love shoes and anything to do with shoes. I figured I could start an online shoe store selling shoes to women like myself. At the same time, I would be able to get shoes for myself at wholesale prices. Why not? I decided on an online business as opposed to a store front for several reasons. I had a full time 9 to 5 job. Therefore, there was no way that I would have the time necessary to run a store. Also, there would have been a lot more money required to open an actual store. Lastly, I wanted a business that could make passive income. In other words, I wanted to make money while I slept. That is the beauty in an online business. Sales can be made as you sleep which means you are literally making money in your sleep. Not only that, sales are being made while you're at the market or while you're on vacation lying on the beach sipping on a fruity drink. Also, when you have an online store or business, it allows you to work on other goals hat you may have. Now I do not want to discourage anyone who is focusing on opening a physical store. Each individual has their own goals and dreams. Some people are very hands on and enjoy working with people, and an online store may not be the best option for them. Which ever you prefer, an online store or a store front, all of the guidelines that I provide in this book will apply to both. Now getting back to when I first started Divalynn Shoetique. I was nervous and afraid. I was afraid to invest not only the money, but the time and energy required. To put all of my time, energy, and money into this just to lose it, was a scary thought. I started my online shoe business with roughly two thousand dollars. Which is not a lot of money, but it is a lot of money to watch go down the toilet. Then I read a quote by Monkey D. Luffy that read "If you don't take risks, you can't create a future". So that's what I did, I took the risk. I launched Divalynn Shoetique on May 30, 2017, within three months, I got back the two thousand dollars that I invested and more (See image on following page of my August 2017 sales numbers).

📅 Aug 1–Aug 31, 2017

compared to Jul 1–Jul 31, 2017

Total sales

$5,453.48   ↑ 7,576%

Online Store
$5,453.48   ↑ 7,576%

SALES OVER TIME

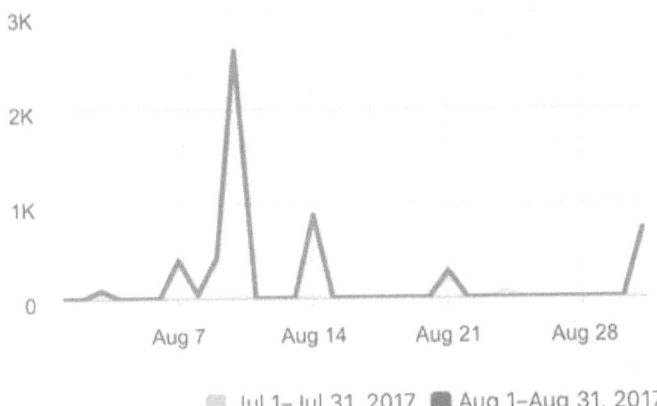

Fast forward to a year and a half later, Divalynn Shoetique is still up and running. While working on my online store, I am also able to work as a successful Real Estate Agent. In addition to that, while writing this book, I started a Life Coaching business. I completed an online life coaching course and I started my business, Coach Belinda Blanding.

My website information will be posted at the end of this book. I wanted to start a life coaching business for the same reason I wrote this book. I love to help people and share my knowledge and experiences. I want to help assist people with living their lives to the fullest. To be all that they can be. To find out what they want for their lives and what's holding them back from getting it. With this business I will be conducting one on one sessions clients to discuss how I can help them. I will also be available for hired speaking engagements. Lastly, I will also be conducting live webinars where I will discuss various topics and answer questions asked by clients. One of the webinars will be on starting a business. I will be discussing every thing that I discuss in this book. The difference is it will be live and you'd be able to ask questions and have them answered live .

Now I have created two businesses of my own. Two very different businesses. One is a business that provides a product, the other is a business that provides a service. Remember I talked about the different types of business earlier. Both required the same steps to get started that I mentioned in this book. Both needed a to have a business structure set up, both needed to be registered, and both have a domain and website. The reason why I sharing this with you is to encourage you and let you know that you don't have to limit yourself. You can have one business, five businesses, or anything in between. How ever many you can handle. Never ever rely on one source of income. The more the better. Did you know that the average millionaire has seven streams of income? Yes seven. I have two and I am no where near done yet. I plan on starting a Real Estate business one day. That would be much later on. I also plan on starting other businesses in the near future. I don't want you to get overwhelmed with the thought of multiple businesses. Just keep in mind for later on down the line that you don't have to limit yourself. For now we will stay focused on getting you started on your first business.

CHAPTER 8
KEEP PUSHING

Ready? Let's Go! It is going to be a bumpy ride so put on your seatbelts. I am going to tell you now, if you are not a risk taker, if you are not willing to put in the work, or if you are expecting success overnight, entrepreneurship is not the life for you. There will be a lot of late nights and early mornings. You will also be giving up your weekends a lot of times. In order to succeed you will have to make those sacrifices and more. It will take a lot of patience and discipline on your part. Again, do not expect success overnight. Every business is different. You cannot compare the success of anther business to the success or lack of success of yours. The average new business can take two to three years, or longer to become profitable. If it takes yours a little longer, do not give up. You will be closer to success than you think. Keep putting in the work daily and I assure you, you will reap the benefits. I cannot emphasize that enough. You must work on the success of your business every single day consistently. With consistency, hard work and dedication, your business will flourish. Your dream will only work if you work. As an entrepreneur, there is no forty hour a week work shift. Be prepared to work double that some weeks. You will have to work hard even when you don't feel like it. There is no calling in sick to the boss when you don't feel well. You are the boss! There are no days off. The day that you decided to become an entrepreneur, this is what you signed up for. This is what comes with holding the entrepreneur title.

There will be many days when you will feel like giving up and throwing in the towel, trust me I know. That is when you should think of the reason that you started in the first place. Go back to the question that I asked you to write the answer to earlier . Look at your whys. Looking at your whys will get you back focused and motivated. At least that is what it has done for me whenever I have had those feelings of quitting. Even now, I sometimes feel discouraged when sales drop. Then I think of my whys and come up with a new campaign idea, or something that will help to get new customers and boost sales. I suggest you keep your list of whys handy and in a safe place. You will be needing it for years to come. Always look back on it. Not only when you feel like quitting, but also for those days when you just need a little motivation and inspiration. There will be lots of ups and downs. Any entrepreneur will tell you this. There will be days when you feel like you've won the lottery. Then there will be days when you feel like

"What did I get myself into?". Being an entrepreneur is not all glamours and perfect as we make it appear to be. We have our low periods. The days when business is slow or there's no business at all. But no entrepreneur is going to go shouting from the top of the building that business is slow or doing bad. It.is human nature to highlight the highs of the business, not the lows. There will be times when you may put in a lot of hours working on improvements, you may spend a lot of money on marketing, all to no avail. Which can be very frustrating and not to mention, discouraging. There will be times when it will seem like nothing is going right and everything is going wrong. There will be times that nothing will go as planned. Again, keep pushing and do not give up. This is all normal with any new business. These things happen and those feelings of frustration and discouragement come and go. This is what comes with the territory of being an entrepreneur. The most important thing is to not become consumed with those feelings and keep pushing. You have to be confident and believe in your business and believe in your product or service. If you don't believe in you, no one else will. You will already have plenty of doubters. You don't need to prove them right by doubting yourself as well. When times get hard, and when things are not happening they way you expected, then and only then, will you be able to determine if the life of an entrepreneur is the life for you. As an entrepreneur, you must be consider certain things. A quick example is, unless you have a consistent reliable income coming in from another source, you will be living off of fluctuating income. Remember business will be up and down. Some months you may bring in lots of profit and some months you may not bring in any. You have to ask yourself if that is something that you can handle. If not, I advise that you do not resign from your current job until you are financially comfortable enough to do so. The life of an entrepreneur can be very rewarding but you reap what you sow. The more work you put in, the more consistent you are, and as long as you never give up, all of the lows will be well worth the highs. After all of the rain you will see the sun finally come out and stay out. You just have to be strong enough to endure the struggle that comes along with it. One day you'll look back and thank yourself for never giving up. You will have a successful business that you will make good money from. You will be able to live the life of your dreams and do all the things you've ever wanted to do. You'll come and go as you please and be able to take vacation whenever and for however long. You will finally be able to experience the rewarding side of entrepreneurship.

CHAPTER 9
MARKETING

In this chapter I will be going over the different ways that you can market your business. Your business is now up and running and you are excited to start doing business. However, you are a new business that no one knows about. The first thing you need to do is make every one that you aware that you now have a business. Word of mouth is always a good way to advertise your business. Let your friends, family members, co-workers, neighbors, anyone that you can think of know about. Then ask them to let everyone that they know know about it. This is the fastest and easiest way to get the word out.

Another idea is to have a launching party. If you are opening a store or a boutique, you can announce the date and invite people to attend. I would recommend some type of incentive such as twenty percent off of their first purchase as well as serving snacks and beverages at the launching party. If you have an online business. You can also make an announcement about the launching date and you may want to create a launching sale as well. Something like thirty percent off of first order use code "launch" at checkout. You know something like that.

In this era, social media plays a huge part in marketing. It is also a way to get your business out there and become known. If you do not have a social media account, I highly recommend getting one. You can just have it for business purposes only if you're not interested in a personal account. With social media you will reach a higher number of potential clients or customers. After setting up your business, I suggest that you open up a couple of social media accounts. I recommend Instagram and Facebook. Once you open up the accounts send out follow requests to everyone you know. Then ask that they send requests to everyone that they know to follow you. Before you know it, you will have a large amount of followers. The benefit of having a large amount of followers is that they will all see the content that you post. You can post your products, advertisements, etc. Anything that you want people to know about your business you can post on your social media page. Your location, your website information, or anything that you want. The more followers that you have, the more potential customers/clients you will have. When posting on social media, here are a few tips you may want to follow for best results:

* Post quality content - make sure pictures are clear and not blurry.

* Post daily - Posting daily all keep your followers interest and will keep new ones coming.
* Make sure that the content that you are sharing has an appealing appearance.
* Communicate with your followers by replying to their comments. Let them know that you are not above having a conversation with them.
* Grab their attention by offering discounts. Especially when you first launch your business. It gives them the incentive to check out your business and hopefully become a customer.

Another way of marketing on social media, other than just posting is doing campaign ads. This is when you pay a certain amount of money to have facebook and/or instagram run your ad for a certain number of day. For example, lets say you just got a new arrival of products that you want to advertise. You would create the post on your business page, then after its posted, you will have the option of promoting the post. You will see a button that says "Promote" if on Instagram or "Boost Post" if on facebook. Once you click on the button you will be able to choose how much money you would like to spend. For example if you choose to spend twenty dollars. You will choose twenty dollars. Then choose how many days. It can be something like four days at five dollars per day, two days at ten dollars per day, or one day for the whole twenty dollars. The more spent per day increases the number of people that will see your ad that day.

Email marketing is another great way to market your business. Once you start doing business, you will have a record of your customers. If you have an online business, when the customer orders online they will automatically be asked for their email address. If you have any other type of business, you may want to consider asking each customer for their email address and keep a record of all of them. This is for the purpose of email marketing. Email marketing is when you send one email blast. An email that is sent out to all of your customers at once. You can send an email blast to inform customers of new arrivals, upcoming sales, or any news about your business. Email marketing is my favorite type of marketing because they have done business with you before, therefore, they are more trusting of you and more likely to purchase from you again. I recommend using Mailchimp for your email marketing. If you are starting an online business, and set up your online store through Shopify, "Kit" is also great for email marketing. Kit is a free marketing tool for Shopify users. Kit also does campaign ads, social media posts, and a lot more. I highly recommend using Kit if you will by using Shopify.

Lastly, be your own walking advertisement. Every person that you speak to is a potential customer or client. If someone strikes up a conversation with you, use that as an opportunity to bring up your business and leave them with your business card. You should initiate conversations as well. Strike up conversations with as many people as possible. The lady sitting next to you in the nail salon, the guy sitting next to you in the barber, the person sitting next to you on the train, etc. Don't be shy. After striking up a conversation, Kindly hand them your business card. I would usually say something like "Whenever you need a cute pair of shoes, check out my website" as I hand them the card. If it's a man, I would say, "If you ever want to buy your significant other a nice pair of shoes check me out", something like that. Put yourself out there daily. People won't know about y unless you tell them about you. Also, when I say be your own walking advertisement, I mean that literally as well. When I sold Mary Kay, I walked around wearing a Mary Kay pin on my blouse or blazer and I carried a Mary Kay tote bag. There were many times that people came up to me telling me that they have been looking for a Mary Kay representative and couldn't find one, or that the person that they usually order from no longer sells it. Just by me carrying the bag or wearing a pin, I attracted new customers. You can also do things like ordering T-shirts with your business name and have customized tote bags made with your business name on it. Wear the t-shirt and carry the tote bag as often as possible. That is a sure way to start up conversations about your business. For my online store, I have a sticker on my car's bumper with the name and website of my business. That has gained me new customers as well. Advertise your business as many ways as you possibly can.

If you incorporate all of the above tips into your marketing strategy, I guarantee you will build your clientele as well as build your business. Marketing is a very important factor in the success of your business. Please take it seriously and invest the time, energy, and money necessary. It will be well worth it in the end.

RESOURCES TO KEEP HANDY

* DOMAINE NAME AND EMAIL: **GODADDY**
* SETTING UP LEGAL STRUCTURE/BUSINESS LICENSING/REGISTER BUSINESS NAME: **LEGAL ZOOM**
*BUSINESS PLANS/LOANS/INVESTORS: **SMALL BUSINESS ADMINISTRATION (SBA)**
* ACCOUNTING SOFTWARE: **XERO**
* EMAIL MARKETING: **MAILCHIMP**
* DIY GRAPHIC DESIGNS: **CANVA**
* LOGOS: **99 DESIGNS**
* BUSINESS CARDS/STATIONERY/MARKETING SUPPLIES: **VISTA PRINT**

EPILOGUE

In this step by step guide to starting a business, I have put together all of the details needed based on my own research and personal experiences and knowledge. With this guide, you will have all of the necessary tools and knowledge to start and run the business that you have always wanted to. I have given you all of the resources that you need to go forward from here. Now it is up to you to put them to use. My one and only objective was to share my knowledge and to motivate others like myself who know that they were not put on this earth to be mediocre. I believe that I have done just that. Wishing you all of the success in the world.

- Belinda Blanding

www.ingramcontent.com/pod-product-compliance
Lightning Source LLC
Chambersburg PA
CBHW030940240526
45463CB00015B/860